ABOUT
MYTHS AND LEGENDS

PUBLISHER	Joseph R. DeVarennes	
PUBLICATION DIRECTOR	Kenneth H. Pearson	
ADVISORS	Roger Aubin	
	Robert Furlonger	
EDITORIAL SUPERVISOR	Jocelyn Smyth	
PRODUCTION MANAGER	Ernest Homewood	
PRODUCTION ASSISTANTS	Martine Gingras	Kathy Kishimoto
	Catherine Gordon	Peter Thomlison
CONTRIBUTORS	Alison Dickie	Nancy Prasad
	Bill Ivy	Lois Rock
	Jacqueline Kendel	Merebeth Switzer
	Anne Langdon	Dave Taylor
	Sheila Macdonald	Alison Tharen
	Susan Marshall	Donna Thomson
	Pamela Martin	Pam Young
	Colin McCance	
SENIOR EDITOR	Robin Rivers	
EDITORS	Brian Cross	Ann Martin
	Anne Louise Mahoney	Mayta Tannenbaum
PUBLICATION ADMINISTRATOR	Anna Good	
ART AND DESIGN	Richard Comely	Ronald Migliore
	George Elliott	Sue Wilkinson
	Greg Elliott	

Canadian Cataloguing in Publication Data

Main entry under title:

Questions kids ask about myths and legends

(Questions kids ask ; 16)
ISBN 0-7172-2555-0

1. Mythology—Miscellanea—Juvenile literature.
2. Legends—Miscellanea—Juvenile literature.
3. Children's questions and answers.
I. Smyth, Jocelyn.   II. Comely, Richard.   III. Series.

BL311.Q47 1988   j291.1'3   C89-093166-6

Questions Kids Ask . . .
about MYTHS AND LEGENDS

continued

What is a legend?

Legends tell about the lives of human beings. Some are based on real people and events, such as the legends of Davy Crockett and (maybe) King Arthur. As people tell and re-tell the story, the original facts are embroidered, making it almost impossible to tell truth from fiction.

Other legends tell of completely imaginary characters. Such are the tall tales of Paul Bunyan—though it is possible that the idea for these began with the feats of an unusually strong lumberjack.

The legends of any society reflect its attitudes and ideals. Their heroes have qualities the society feels are important: courage, intelligence, honesty, strength. Books and films keep these legends alive. They also help create new ones.

What is a myth?

What makes the sun rise? Why do the seasons change? These were questions people long ago asked themselves about the world. They had no scientific answers, so they made up stories, or myths, to help make their world more understandable and less frightening.

Myths take place in a world before ordinary time and describe the lives of supernatural beings, or gods.

Some tell of the origin of the world, the creation of man and the birth of gods and goddesses. Others give a reason for natural processes or events. Thunder and lightning were the weapons used by Zeus, the king of the Greek gods.

Why have ancient myths lasted so long? They are dramatic and exciting stories, and they tell universal truths about human nature that we recognize in ourselves even today.

Who was Demeter?

Demeter was the Greek goddess of the harvest. It was said that no vegetables, grain or fruit could grow without her smile.

One day her daughter, Persephone, was stolen by Hades and taken to his underground kingdom. Demeter wept, and the fields became barren and cold.

When Demeter swore she would not make the earth green again until her daughter was with her, Zeus agreed to let Persephone return for six months of each year. The other six months she would have to spend with Hades.

Every year when Persephone left her, Demeter grieved and nothing grew. There was winter on the earth. But kind Demeter didn't want humans to starve, so she taught them to sow seeds in the spring, harvest in the fall and store food to last the winter.

Who had snakes for hair?

Medusa, a beautiful girl in ancient Greece, was so proud of her lovely hair that she challenged a goddess to a beauty contest. This angered the goddess who punished Medusa by turning her into a monster. Medusa's ringlets became a mass of writhing snakes. Her body became covered with hard scales, and her beautiful face became so frightful that anyone who looked at her turned to stone!

Medusa fled to a far island. All around her cave stood silent

figures of people and animals who had caught a glimpse of her and been turned to stone.

Perseus finally rid the world of the snake-haired Medusa by a clever trick. Using Athena's polished shield as a mirror, he guided himself to Medusa's cave by watching the reflection in it. Carefully, he approached her without looking directly at her. When he heard the serpents hissing, he raised his sword and cut off her head!

Was there a real Robin Hood?

No one has ever proved that there was a real Robin Hood, but there may well have been a man—or several men—who had adventures like those in the stories. The name first comes up in ballads that were written over 600 years ago. Later versions place Robin Hood in different times and in different parts of England, but all of them tell the same basic story of a bold outlaw who lives in the

forest with a merry band of followers, stealing from the rich to give to the poor.

In the version best known to us, Robin lives in Sherwood Forest. He is an excellent archer and he is trustworthy and humorous. His arch-enemy is the greedy and evil sheriff of Nottingham, and his band of followers includes Friar Tuck, Little John, Will Scarlet and the beautiful Maid Marion.

Whether or not there was an actual man named Robin Hood, the ballads were popular and the stories survived and grew because they expressed the wishes of a lot of people. Even today people still enjoy hearing stories about Robin Hood. Sixty stories, 30 plays and a number of operas and movies have been written about him.

What made the unicorn so special?

At first glance he looks like a small, white horse. Then you notice the single, spiral horn in the middle of his forehead, and you know you are looking at a unicorn.

The horn is the unicorn's special strength and power. Legend says that if a unicorn stirred a pool of stagnant water with his horn, it became pure and sweet. Hunters tracked the unicorn for his horn, which they believed was a cure for poison.

But the unicorn was strong and fierce—no hunter could take him by force. Only a young, innocent girl could tame him. So clever hunters would leave a young girl in the woods. When the unicorn saw her, he would run up, rest his head in her lap and sleep. Then the hunters would appear and capture him.

You will find the unicorn in the art and literature of many countries. But the only way to capture him is in your dreams.

10

Who was Pegasus?

You may have seen pictures of a beautiful white horse, rising into the air with outstretched wings. This is Pegasus. He had a very unusual birth—the Greeks say that when Perseus cut off Medusa's snaky head, the winged horse sprang up from Medusa's blood soaking into the earth.

The goddess Athena gave the young warrior Bellerophon a golden bridle so he could tame the winged horse.

Bellerophon mounted Pegasus, rose into the air and destroyed the Chimaera, a fire-breathing monster.

Bellerophon had many adventures, and with the help of Pegasus, he always triumphed. Finally, he became so proud that he tried to fly to heaven on his winged horse. Angered, the gods sent a gadfly to sting Pegasus. Bellerophon was thrown to the earth, and Pegasus flew on alone through the sky where he became a constellation.

Who was the goddess of wisdom?

The Greek goddess Athena (or Minerva as the Romans called her) came from a most suitable place for a goddess of wisdom—her father's head! She sprang from the head of Zeus, father of the gods, full grown, dressed in a helmet and armor. Although she had no love of war, she often led armies, but only those that fought for just causes. When her favorites were in trouble, Athena would shield them with a cloud. She often appeared to humans in dreams and gave them advice.

Athena entered a city-naming contest with Poseidon, god of the sea, the winner to be the god that gave the most useful gift to humans. Poseidon gave them the horse. Athena gave the olive tree, which supplies food, oil and wood. Athena won, and the city was named Athens in her honor. Under her leadership, the Athenians became famous for their skill in the arts and sciences.

DID YOU KNOW . . . the planet Mars was given that name because its reddish glow looked like blood.

What sort of god was Mars?

Mars, the Roman god of war, is usually portrayed in armor, wearing a crested helmet. When he heard the clashing of arms, Mars grunted with glee, leaped into his war chariot and rushed into the thick of the battle. He didn't care who won or lost, as long as much blood was shed. Mars was boastful and hot-tempered—always looking for a fight. Venus, the goddess of love, admired Mars for his good looks, but none of the other gods were very fond of him.

Who was god of the sea?

Poseidon, the Greek god of the sea (Neptune to the Romans) was the brother of Zeus. He carried a three-pronged spear, or trident, which was his symbol of power. He was also called Earth-shaker because of his habit of splitting mountains with his trident and rolling them into the sea to become islands. Tempests raged when Poseidon struck the sea in anger. When he stretched out his hand, the sea grew calm again.

Poseidon had a glittering palace in the depths of the Aegean Sea, but he was rarely at home. He was a restless god, always racing off in his chariot, pulled by a team of snow-white horses. Whales and dophins frolicked as he passed by, and the sea opened before him as his chariot flew across the waves.

DID YOU KNOW . . . the Greeks say that Poseidon created the horse by striking the ground with his trident.

What was Rip Van Winkle famous for?

What's the longest you've ever slept? Half a day? A whole day? Well, Rip Van Winkle slept so long it could only happen in a legend.

Rip was a simple man, who lived in the Catskill Mountains of New York long ago. One day, Rip took his gun and his dog into the mountains to hunt. When it was getting dark, a little man appeared in old-fashioned clothes, with a keg on his back. He gestured to Rip to help him, which Rip did gladly, and together they climbed higher up the mountain. There they met a group of little men bowling. The men never spoke but motioned to Rip to serve them the drink in the keg. He did—and drank quite a bit himself. Then he fell asleep.

When Rip woke up, his gun was rusty, his dog had disappeared and his beard had grown down to his waist. He headed home, only to find that his house was in ruins, his wife had died and the village was full of strangers. He had slept for 20 years!

Who was Davy Crockett?

Davy Crockett was born in the backwoods of Tennessee in 1786. He had a brief political career but is best known as a hunter, scout and soldier.

A humorist, Crockett loved to write and tell tall tales about himself. Other writers exaggerated these stories and he became a folk hero during his lifetime.

Crockett died fighting in the battle of the Alamo to help free Texas from Mexico.

14

What did Paul Bunyan do?

The tall tales of Paul Bunyan begin with his birth. His cradle, they say, was too big for the land so it floated in the ocean. One day the huge baby bounced up and down and caused a tidal wave!

Paul Bunyan grew to be a giant lumberjack who could break a tall pine tree in half with his bare hands. He could outrun the swiftest deer and cross the widest river in one stride. And he could chop down a whole forest in a single day.

A giant man needed giant tools. Paul's axe was as wide as a barn door and had a great oak tree for a handle. It took six grown men to lift it.

His companion, Babe the Blue Ox, was almost as big as Paul, and took part in his amazing adventures.

It was said that Paul Bunyan cut the Grand Canyon by dragging his pick behind him. Another story is told of how Paul and his men dug the St. Lawrence River on a bet in just three weeks! Some say he even logged the moon.

His legend still lives today. When lumberjacks find small lakes, they say they are the footprints of Paul Bunyan that have filled up with water.

What was in Pandora's box?

The Greeks say that Pandora was the first woman. When she was created, the gods gave her all possible gifts: beauty, intelligence, every talent. They also gave her a closed box that she was warned never, never to open.

The box stood in her room, so Pandora saw it every day. At first she resisted the temptation to open it but finally her curiosity became too great. She just had to peek. She lifted the lid . . . and out flew all the things that make people's lives miserable: war, illness, sorrow, anger, greed. They spread like dark shadows across the earth. Terrified, Pandora shut the lid, but the box was almost empty. Only hope lay at the bottom. So if you are bothered by one of the troubles that escaped from Pandora's box, just remember that there is always hope.

Who was the goddess of love?

The birth of Venus, the Roman goddess of love and beauty (the Greeks called her Aphrodite), is as strange and beautiful as the goddess herself. The story is that she sprang from the white foam of the sea! The west wind gently blew her in a scallop shell across the water to the island of Cyprus.

The gods were charmed by her gleaming fair hair, her silvery feet, her graceful figure and her sweet smile. Each wished to have her for his wife. Surprisingly, although Venus was attracted to several of them—and to some humans too—she chose to marry Vulcan, the ugliest god of them all.

What did Cupid use his arrows for?

Cupid is usually pictured as a chubby, naked boy with wings, holding a bow and arrow. According to myth, when Cupid shoots one of his magical arrows into your heart, you fall instantly in love with the first person you see.

Cupid's mother was Venus, the goddess of love. She gave him his bow and quiver of arrows. The arrows of love had tips of gold and Cupid delighted in shooting them into the hearts of people and gods, causing them to fall in love. However, Cupid was a mischievous boy and sometimes caused no end of trouble by shooting his arrows at the wrong people!

DID YOU KNOW . . . some of Cupid's arrows had tips of lead? When he shot these at someone's heart, they produced the opposite feelings—hatred and dislike.

Who was Achilles?

Achilles' mother was a sea nymph who wanted to give her baby the gift of immortality. She dipped him in the Styx, the river of the underworld. This made Achilles injury-proof—except for one heel by which his mother held him.

During the Trojan War, Achilles killed Hector to avenge a dear friend's death. Hector's brother then managed to shoot an arrow into Achilles' heel—his only weak spot—and kill him.

We now use the term ''Achilles' heel'' to mean any special area of weakness a person has.

Who was Hercules?

Although he was the son of Zeus, Hercules had many failings. The Greeks didn't like their heroes to be perfect, and Hercules was no exception. According to the tales, he was the strongest of all men but he wasn't overly bright. He also had a very short and violent temper, which caused him to murder his own wife and children. This evil deed was done under a spell of madness put on him by Hera, Zeus' jealous wife (who was not Hercules' mother). Hercules thought that he should make up for such a terrible deed, so he undertook 12 seemingly impossible tasks. They are known as the ''Labors of Hercules.'' The first task was to kill a fierce lion. The next was to kill a nine-headed creature called Hydra. Then Hercules had to capture a wild boar and a stag with golden horns. He succeeded in the rest of his 12 tasks and went on to many other strange and wonderful adventures.

What was Atlas famous for?

Atlas is the hero of strong men. He was a Titan, or giant, and so strong that he could hold up the earth! In the early days of Greece, the Titans fought against the Olympian gods and lost. So the gods punished Atlas by forcing him to support the world on his shoulders forever.

Atlas bore this great burden for many years until Hercules came by, seeking help in one of his labors—getting golden apples for the king from a tree guarded by a dragon. Atlas agreed to get the apples if Hercules held up the world while he was gone.

Atlas was so happy to be free of his burden that after he got the golden apples, he told Hercules he intended to take them to the king himself. Hercules pretended to agree but asked Atlas to hold the world for a moment while he padded his shoulders with a lion skin to ease the strain. Then he shifted the world back onto Atlas' shoulders, picked up the apples and left.

WHEW

OH HERC... **HERC!**

19

Is there such a thing as a werewolf?

If you mean a person who turns into a wolf at night and goes around killing and eating people, the answer is no. So where did the idea come from?

Long ago in Scandinavia, there was a very fierce group called Berserkers. They raided towns wearing animal skins that made them look like wolves or bears in human form.

Then there is a mental disease where people think they are animals. They may growl, run around on all fours and crave raw meat. There is also a rare genetic disease (passed on from parent to child) where long, silky hair appears *all* over the body.

Any or all these things may explain why some people long ago believed in creatures who were humans by day and wolves by night.

Are there really witches?

There really were people who called themselves witches (in fact there still are) but they weren't necessarily ugly and they didn't fly around on broomsticks.

The word *witch* comes from "wicca," meaning wise. The first witches were men and women who became wise in the ways of nature and used their skills to heal others.

But because they had unusual abilities, ordinary people were a little afraid of them. If they could heal in what seemed mysterious ways, wasn't it likely they could also injure . . . ?

And so the idea of evil witches

was born and grew, encouraged by early church leaders who disapproved of witches because they worked outside the church.

How did legends about vampires begin?

Vampire! You immediately think of coffins and graveyards and the pale man—the undead—who sleeps by day and comes out at night. His eye-teeth are longer and more pointed than normal, so he can bite into your veins because he wants to suck your blood and make you a vampire too.

Are you terrified? Don't be: there is no such thing as a real vampire. But there have been people who were so bloodthirsty and cruel that simple folk couldn't believe they were completely human. It was

probably stories about the evil acts of such people that grew into vampire legends.

One such person was Prince Vlad, born in 1430 in Transylvania, (now a part of Romania). He was called "dracul," meaning devil, because he murdered thousands of people in particularly cruel ways. Bram Stoker used him as a model for the vampire in his famous book, *Dracula*.

DID YOU KNOW . . . people believed that garlic would scare away vampires but that the only way to kill one was to drive a stake through its heart.

21

Was there a place called Atlantis?

The legend of Atlantis began with the Greek philosopher Plato. He told a story about a vast continent that sank beneath the ocean in one awful night. He called this continent Atlantis.

For a long time people thought that Plato's story was true. But today people think that the story of the drowned continent is only a legend. The continents we live on were under water at one time, but that was millions of years ago. Scientists who have studied the Atlantic Ocean say that its bottom has been under water for millions of years.

There are new theories that Atlantis was an island lost under the Mediterranean Sea. An island south of Greece named Thira was destroyed in a mighty volcanic eruption a thousand years before Plato wrote his story, and some people think Thira was Atlantis.

Where was Valhalla?

According to Norse mythology, a warrior who died bravely in battle didn't stop feasting and fighting when he died. He was whisked away over the rainbow bridge to Valhalla to revel with Odin, king of the gods, in his mountaintop palace.

Valhalla was a huge hall, glittering with gold. The dead heroes sat at long tables, feasting on boar's meat and telling stories of their courage. Every morning, they rode out to fight and play war-like games.

Who was the Flying Dutchman?

Wrong question! The *Flying Dutchman* isn't a "who" at all but a "what."

According to one of the greatest sea legends of all time, the *Flying Dutchman* is a phantom ship that haunts the seas off the Cape of Good Hope in South Africa and is seen in stormy weather. The story is told that the captain murdered someone on board the ship and because of this he and his crew are doomed to sail the seas eternally—without ever coming to port.

Another version says that the captain is still trying to make good an oath he swore to round the cape even if it took forever. A German legend adds that the captain spends his time playing dice with the devil for possession of his soul.

Whatever the story, a sighting of this ship is said to foretell disaster.

Were there ever dragons?

Dragons have stalked through folklore since ancient times. Dragons don't really exist, but most people in the ancient world believed in them. In fact, early maps showed unexplored lands as the places where dragons lived.

Most folklores describe dragons as fierce fire-breathing serpents that can burn you to ashes with one powerful puff of flames. They can swallow people or entire ships in one gulp, and kidnap beautiful maidens.

In Christian countries, dragons were for a long time the symbol of evil, and the test of a person's courage and faith was to slay one of these huge beasts.

DID YOU KNOW . . . in Chinese folklore, dragons represented gods. It was good luck to run into a dragon in China.

EEK! A MONSTER!

Is there really a Loch Ness monster?

Mystery surrounds the narrow Scottish lake called Loch Ness. For almost 1500 years people have claimed that a monster with a huge body and a head like a snake lives in it.

Photographs have even shown what looks to be a large snake-like head sticking out of the water. These can be explained away, but the tales persist.

Is there really a monster, perhaps a relative of the dinosaurs, in Loch Ness? Until we have more proof, all we can say is that maybe there is.

What are mermaids?

Stories about mermaids probably started when sailors saw sea mammals called manatees and dugongs.

Manatees and dugongs look like seals, but when they nurse their young they hold the babies to their breasts with their front flippers. Seen from a distance, they look almost like human mothers. It was this habit that gave rise the the tales of beautiful creatures that are half-women, half-fish.

Was there a real King Arthur?

Very likely there was. But the stories we read and love about his court at Camelot, and his brave and courteous knights are almost entirely fiction.

The legend of Arthur belongs to those early inhabitants of the British Isles who are now called the Welsh. In the 400s and the 500s, they were conquered by Saxon invaders. The original Arthur may have been a king, or he may have just been a very brave man who led his people in resisting the Saxons.

Although legend tells us that Arthur and his knights won 12 battles and he killed 960 men single-handedly, the Welsh were finally driven out of most of Britain. As time passed they became Christian, and somehow tales about Arthur became mixed up with stories about the gods the Welsh had had before. Familiar tales about King Arthur include those of his education by the magician Merlin, his removing the sword Excalibur from the stone to prove he was the King of England, and the adventures of Lancelot and

Galahad and the other knights of the Round Table.

Arthur and his knights became and have remained great popular heroes. Writers today are still finding new ways to retell the tales and attaching new meanings to them.

Who was Merlin?

Merlin was a mysterious figure in the legends of ancient England. He was called a wizard, a prophet and a magician. His mother was a mortal, but people believed that Merlin's special powers came from his father, who was one of the fairy folk.

Merlin grew up wild in the forest, learning the secrets of nature and the language of animals. He could change himself into any shape he pleased: a dwarf, an old man, a deer or a tree. He could even make himself invisible.

Merlin played an important part in the legend of King Arthur and his knights. Merlin raised Arthur and kept him safe until it was time for him to take the throne. Merlin often had visions of the future and used them to advise the king.

In old age, Merlin was tricked by a wicked enchantress and locked in a cave. And there, some say, he still sleeps, waiting to be released.

Is there really an Abominable Snowman?

Signs of a large, hairy creature that looks half-ape, half-human have been reported from the Himalayan to the Rocky Mountains. (In the Rockies it is known as the Sasquatch or Bigfoot.) These signs have consisted most often of footprints, which scientists claim could only have been made by a very large creature that walks upright. There have also been hair samples found from time to time, and police labs have been unable to identify them as belong to any known animal. Finally, there are many people in different parts of the world who say they have seen such a creature. The Sherpa people who live in the Himalayas believe in the Abominable Snowman, and their government officially recognizes and "protects" it.

Thus there is some evidence that the Abominable Snowman exists. But no one has captured one or even produced photos that clearly could not have been faked. Maybe you'll be the one to solve the mystery.

DID YOU KNOW . . . people looking for the Abominable Snowman found footprints 36 centimetres (14 inches) long!

28

DID YOU KNOW . . . the unicorn legend may have started when someone saw a rhinoceros for the first time.

What is a centaur?

This strange creature is half man and half horse! It has the head, arms and torso of a man, and the legs and body of a horse. Historians think that the idea of the centaur began when ancient tribes first saw a man on horseback and thought the two were joined together.

Most centaurs were brutal—as cunning as foxes and as savage as untamed horses. Centaurs mingled with humans, but were difficult to tame because they hated law and order.

One centaur, Chiron, was different from other centaurs. He was skilled in hunting, healing, music and art, and he became one of the greatest teachers in Greece. Since he was also wise and kind, kings brought their small sons to Chiron so they could learn how to become wise and courageous. Chiron taught so many important Greek heroes that, at his death, he was honored by being placed among the stars as the constellation Sagittarius.

What was the riddle of the Sphinx?

The Sphinx was a fabulous creature found in Egyptian and Greek myths. In Egypt it had the body of a lion and the face of the pharaoh, or king. Greeks believed the Sphinx had the face and bust of a woman, a lion's body and the wings of a bird.

A Greek myth tells the story of the Sphinx which was sent by the gods to the city of Thebes to ask all travelers a riddle. Those who solved the riddle could pass by safely, but those who failed were devoured. Since no one knew the answer, many were killed.

Then the hero Oedipus came along and the Sphinx asked him: "What animal goes on four feet in the morning, on two feet at noon and on three feet in the evening?" Oedipus answered, "It is a man. In childhood he creeps on hands and knees; in manhood, he walks erect on two feet; in old age he supports himself with a stick."

On hearing the correct answer, the Sphinx threw herself from the rock and died. The people of Thebes were so grateful to Oedipus for saving them from the Sphinx that they made him their king.

DID YOU KNOW . . . a colossal stone sphinx standing 21 metres (66 feet) high was built nearly 5000 years ago and can be seen today in the desert near the pyramids at Giza, in Egypt.

What has an eagle's wings, a lion's body and a snake's tail?

It's the griffin, one of the most ancient of mythical beasts. People believed it combined the keen vision and swiftness of the eagle with the courage and strength of the lion.

Legends about the griffin vary from country to country, but most agree that it was sacred to the sun, that it lived in the mountains of southern Russia, where it guarded a treasure of gold from the one-eyed Scythians, and that it could never be taken alive. It was so strong and fierce that it could fly off with a man in armor—horse and all!

What is a phoenix?

Can you imagine living for 500 years? Or entering a fire, old and infirm, to emerge strong and newborn? Or being the only one of your kind? All this has been said of the fabulous phoenix, bird of myth and legend.

The phoenix looked like an eagle with gleaming feathers of scarlet and gold. It fed on the light of the sun and was said to live in Arabia. There was only one phoenix alive on earth at any one time, for it gave birth to itself—once every 500 years.

When its body became worn and it could no longer fly as fast as the wind, the phoenix gathered fragrant twigs of cinnamon, frankincense and myrrh and built a nest on top of a tall palm. Then, the twigs were ignited by the sun. The flames rose up and consumed the phoenix, and a new one arose from the ashes of the old!

31

Index _____